T. D. BARTH, MSN, MBA

Essential Leadership Skills

The Path to Effectiveness, Influence, and Growth

First edition

This book was professionally typeset on Reedsy.
Find out more at reedsy.com

"Leadership is not about titles, positions or flowcharts. It is about one life influencing another."

John C. Maxwell

Contents

1

Introduction

A story unfolds daily in the heart of a bustling city amidst the cacophony of daily professional and personal life. It is the story of individuals stepping into roles brimming with potential and challenge. I remember my first day as a new leader - the mixture of pride and anxiety, the weight of responsibility, and the burning question: "Am I ready for this?" This book is born from those early days of leadership, from every triumph and setback to every lesson learned in the management trenches.

Leadership is not just a title or a role; it is a journey of self-discovery and impact. In this role, you are not just overseeing tasks; you are shaping careers, influencing culture, and leaving a lasting impression on the lives of those you lead. This book, "Essentials Leadership Skills: The Path to Effectiveness, Influence, and Growth," is crafted as your compass in this journey. It is not just about what to do but about who you become in the process.

Let us start by unpacking the essence of your leadership role, diving into what it truly means to lead and not just manage. Then, we will explore the core skills that set influential leaders apart - from mastering communication to decision-making, time management, and conflict resolution. Leadership is an art; like all artists, leaders need their tools. You will learn about building and leading teams as groups of individuals working together and as a cohesive unit thriving towards a common goal. Then, navigate through the often-turbulent waters of challenges and conflict, learning to view them not as roadblocks but as stepping stones to greater effectiveness and understanding.

Growth and continuous improvement form the backbone of enduring leadership. The final part of your journey will focus on self-reflection, feedback, and the relentless pursuit of learning. The mark of a great leader is not just in the success they achieve but in the legacy they leave and the paths they pave for others to follow.

I hope you find more than strategies and tips as you turn these pages. Look for a mirror reflecting your potential and a window opening to new horizons. This book is a guide, but the journey is uniquely yours. Embrace it with openness and courage, and watch as the leader within you unfolds, ready to make a mark in the world.

As we transition into the next chapter, "Understanding Your Leadership Role," prepare to dive deep into the essence of what makes a leader, well, a leader. It is a chapter that sets the foundation for everything that follows, ensuring you are not just walking the path of leadership but leaving footprints for others to follow.

2

Understanding The Leadership Role

I magine standing at a crossroads. One path is well-trodden, comfortable, and familiar – the path of the manager. The other, less defined, is the path of a leader. This chapter is about choosing the latter, understanding the profound difference between managing and leading, and embracing the metamorphosis that this choice entails.

The Manager vs. The Leader: A Tale of Two Paths

In the professional growth mindset, few concepts are as pivotal yet frequently misunderstood as the distinction between a manager and a leader. This subtle yet profound difference is the cornerstone of effective leadership.

A manager oversees the execution of tasks. They are the process orchestrators, ensuring that tasks get completed, goals are met, and the day-to-day operations run smoothly. The manager's role is crucial; they ensure the team adheres to deadlines, meets targets, and follows protocols. Their world is one of order, efficiency, and control.

Leadership, however, transcends these functional responsibilities. A leader is more than just a role or a position; it is a mindset and a way of being. While a manager ensures that things are done right, a leader focuses on doing the right things. Here, the leader sets a vision, inspiring and motivating the team and fostering an environment where innovation and creativity are welcomed and encouraged.

As a manager, your role often revolves around organizing, planning, and overseeing tasks. It is a role that calls for efficiency, order, and control. Nevertheless, as a leader, you step into a realm that transcends these boundaries. Leadership is about vision, inspiration, and influence. It is less about what you do and more about what you empower others to achieve. The leader's path is about setting a direction, not just a plan; it is about igniting a sense of purpose, not just assigning tasks.

Understanding this distinction is crucial for anyone stepping into a managerial role. It is about recognizing that your impact extends far beyond tasks and objectives. It is the culture you nurture, the values you instill, and the vision you set forth. In doing so, you transition from a manager overseeing operations to a leader shaping the future.

From Individual Contributor to Inspirational Guide

Transitioning from an individual contributor to a leader represents a fundamental shift in mindset and perspective. It is a journey from working on tasks to inspiring people, from focusing on personal achievements to empowering team success.

As an individual contributor, the primary focus was on the tasks, responsibilities, and performance. Success was measured by how well you completed these assignments and contributed to the team's objectives. This role required specialization, proficiency in specific skills, and a strong sense of personal accountability.

However, stepping into a leadership role demands a broader vision. It is no longer just about your performance but how effectively you can motivate, guide, and elevate the team. This shift in mindset

4

involves looking at the bigger picture and understanding how each team member's strengths can be harnessed for the group's collective success.

Adopting the mindset of a leader means embracing the role of a motivator and a strategist. Instead of diving deep into the details, your job is to provide direction, remove obstacles, and provide an environment for the team to thrive. It is about setting clear goals, providing resources and support, and trusting the team to execute the vision.

Leadership also involves a shift from executing to empowering. It is about recognizing the potential in your team members and helping them realize it. This may mean delegating tasks you used to do yourself, which can be a challenging transition. However, it is essential to remember that empowering the team not only aids their development but also frees you to focus on strategic planning and decision-making.

Remember your days as an individual contributor, the satisfaction of ticking off tasks, and the clarity of defined responsibilities. Transitioning from this individual-focused mindset to one of leadership requires a paradigm shift. Suddenly, your success is not just about your achievements but about how well you can elevate others. As a leader, your role is to be a catalyst for the growth and success of your team. Now, you must shift focus from personal accolades to team accomplishments, from individual goals to collective visions.

The Ripple Effect of Your Leadership

Stepping into a leadership role brings a profound responsibility – the responsibility of influence. Your actions, words, and attitudes as a leader significantly impact team dynamics and your organization's overall culture.

As a leader, every decision you make, how you communicate, and how you handle challenges sets a tone that resonates throughout your team.

Your approach to leadership can foster an environment of trust and collaboration or one of fear and competition. Recognizing this influence is crucial. It means understanding that your leadership style affects not only the operational aspects of your team's work but also their morale, motivation, and overall job satisfaction.

One of the most significant areas of influence is how you manage conflict and handle feedback. Navigating these aspects with empathy, fairness, and transparency will build a culture of open communication and continuous improvement. Conversely, avoiding conflict or not providing constructive feedback can lead to a stagnant environment where problems fester and team members feel undervalued.

Your influence also extends to how you recognize and celebrate achievements. Acknowledging your team's hard work and successes can enhance their sense of belonging and worth. This recognition can come in many forms – from a simple 'thank you' to more formal rewards – but the impact is always profound.

Furthermore, your commitment to growth and development sets an example for your team. By showing that you value learning and self-improvement, you create a culture where personal and professional growth is encouraged and appreciated.

Your leadership is like a pebble thrown into a pond; the ripples are your impact on team dynamics and company culture. Every action you take, every decision you make, sends waves throughout your team. How you handle challenges, celebrate successes, and interact with each team member shapes the culture of your workplace. Creating an environment where creativity flourishes, challenges meet resilience, and each member feels valued and empowered.

Your role as a leader is to steward and nurture the culture with your actions and words. Being keenly aware of the impact of your behavior and choices, you understand that they set the tone for the entire team. Be a role model, not just in productivity and professionalism but also in empathy, integrity, and inspiration.

As we wrap up this chapter, reflect on the leader you aspire to be. Think about the qualities defining great leaders and how you can embody them daily. Remember, leadership is not a title or a position but an ongoing journey of growth, influence, and impact.

The next chapter, "Critical Skills as Instruments," will delve into the core skills that will help you navigate this journey, equipping you with the tools you need to be an effective leader.

3

Critical Skills as Instruments

I n the symphony of leadership, three skills are the most critical instruments – communication, decision-making, and time management. Mastering these skills creates a harmony that uplifts the leader and resonates throughout the team. This chapter is dedicated to fine-tuning these skills, ensuring you can lead with clarity, decisiveness, and balance.

Effective Communication: The Leader's Voice

At the heart of impactful leadership lies the art of effective communication. Mastering this skill is essential for any leader, as it forms the bridge between vision and action, between a leader and their team. Effective communication involves relaying information, inspiring, motivating, and creating a shared understanding.

To communicate effectively, start by being clear and concise in your messaging. Avoid jargon or complex language that might obscure your message. Remember, the goal is to make your vision and expectations understandable to everyone on your team. This clarity not only aids in reducing misunderstandings but also in aligning your team's efforts with organizational goals.

However, effective communication is more than just a one-way street; it is more about listening than speaking. Active listening is the art of paying full attention to the speaker, understanding their message, and responding thoughtfully. This helps gather valuable insights from team members and demonstrates respect and value for their ideas and opinions.

Furthermore, motivational communication is vital to inspiring your team. This involves articulating a compelling vision that excites and energizes your team. Use stories and anecdotes to make your messages more relatable and impactful. People are more engaged and motivated to contribute their best when they understand the' why' behind their work.

Remember also to tailor your communication style to your audience. Different team members may respond better to different types of communication. Some may prefer direct and detailed instructions, while others might thrive with a more high-level overview. Being adaptable in your communication style ensures that your message resonates with everyone.

In the symphony of leadership, three skills are the most critical instruments – communication, decision-making, and time management. Mastering these skills creates a harmony that uplifts the leader and resonates throughout the team. This chapter is dedicated to fine-tuning these skills, ensuring you can lead with clarity, decisiveness, and balance.

Decision-Making Strategies: The Leader's Compass

Effective decision-making is a cornerstone of successful leadership (*Strategies for Effective Decision-Making in Leadership Roles*, n.d.). As a leader, you will be faced with a myriad of decisions, some straightforward, others complex and multifaceted. Developing strategies for making informed and timely decisions is crucial to confidently navigating this aspect of your role.

Gather Information and Analyze Data

Begin by collecting all relevant information and data before making a decision. This process involves gathering facts and figures and seeking input from team members and other stakeholders. An informed decision considers diverse perspectives and different aspects of the issue. Use this data to analyze the situation, looking for patterns, trends, and insights to guide your decision.

Consider the Short-Term and Long-Term Impact

Every decision has both immediate and future consequences. When evaluating options, weigh both the short-term outcomes and the long-term implications. Some decisions may offer quick fixes, while others will not be sustainable in the long run. Conversely, other choices require more effort initially but have more significant benefits over time.

Balance Intuition with Rational Analysis

While data and analysis are critical, consider the value of your intuition. Sometimes, the best decision comes from a gut feeling, especially when you have experience in a similar situation. However, ensure that intuition complements rather than dominates rational analysis. A balanced approach often yields the best outcomes.

Decisiveness and Timeliness

Be decisive once you have all the necessary information and have weighed the options. Procrastination or indecision can be costly and undermine your team's confidence in your leadership. However, this does not mean rushing into decisions without due consideration. Strike a balance between deliberation and action.

Learn from Each Decision

Finally, view each decision as a learning opportunity. Reflect on the outcomes of your decisions – what worked, what did not, and why. This reflection will hone your decision-making skills, making you a more effective and confident leader.

Decision-making is the compass that guides the ship of leadership— making choices that are timely, informed, and aligned with your team's goals and values. To refine this skill, embrace a blend of intuition and analysis. Gather as much relevant information as possible, weigh the pros and cons, and trust your judgment. Decisiveness is about speed and making decisions confidently and clearly, even when uncertain. When decisions do not pan out as expected, view them as learning opportunities, not failures.

Time Management for Leaders: The Leader's Clock

Effective time management for leaders involves balancing between focusing on strategic planning and managing day-to-day responsibilities. This skill is critical, as it ensures not only your productivity but also the efficient functioning of your team.

Prioritize and Delegate

Begin by prioritizing tasks based on their importance and urgency. Identify which tasks require your direct attention and which can be delegated to team members. Delegation is a crucial aspect of leadership time management; it empowers your team, builds trust, and allows you to focus on high-level strategic planning. When delegating, ensure that each team member understands their responsibilities and has the resources they need to succeed.

Set Clear Goals and Deadlines

Effective time management is only possible with clear goals and deadlines. These provide direction and a timeline for you and your team, which helps keep everyone on track. Set realistic, achievable goals for both short-term tasks and long-term projects. Regularly review these goals to ensure they align with the team's and organization's overall objectives.

Balance Strategic Planning with Operational Tasks

As a leader, you must balance high-level strategic planning and the operational tasks that keep your team running. Allocate specific times in your schedule for strategic thinking and planning. This involves setting aside a few hours each week without interruptions, allowing you to focus solely on the bigger picture.

Use Tools and Systems

Leverage technology and organizational systems to streamline tasks and save time. This includes project management software, digital calendars, and communication tools. Tools keep you organized and ensure nothing falls through the cracks.

Regularly Review and Adjust Your Approach

Finally, regularly review your time management approach. What is working well? What could be improved? Be open to adjusting your strategies as needed. Look at changing your daily routine, trying new tools, or reallocating tasks among your team.

Time management for leaders goes beyond personal productivity; it is about strategic planning and prioritization that benefits the entire team. It is juggling the immediate needs of today while keeping an eye on tomorrow's horizon. Accomplishing this involves delegating effectively, setting clear priorities, and knowing when to step back and let your team take the reins. Effective time management also means carving out time for reflection and strategic thinking, ensuring one does not get caught up in the day-to-day but steers the ship towards long-term goals.

As we close this chapter, take a moment to reflect on these essential skills. They are the tools that will help you build a foundation of effective leadership. With them, you can inspire and guide your team toward success, creating a work environment that is productive, positive, and purposeful.

In the next chapter, "Building and Leading Teams," we will explore how to apply these skills to assemble and nurture a team that is not just capable but cohesive and motivated.

4

Building and Leading Teams

The actual test of leadership lies in building and guiding a team. Transforming a group of individuals into a unified entity, all moving towards a shared vision. This chapter is a deep dive into the art of assembling and nurturing an effective, cohesive, motivated team.

Creating a Cohesive Team: The Leader's Ensemble

Building a cohesive team is an essential skill for any leader. It involves more than just grouping individuals together; it is about fostering a sense of unity, purpose, and collaboration. Here are strategies to help you assemble and nurture a team that is strong in individual capabilities and harmonious and synergistic as a unit.

Selecting the Right Team Members

The foundation of a cohesive team lies in selecting the right individuals. When assembling your team, look beyond just skills and experience. Consider how potential team members' personalities, values, and work styles will mesh with the existing team dynamics. Diversity in perspectives and backgrounds can significantly enhance a team's problem-solving ability and creativity. Still, ensuring that all members commit to shared goals and values is crucial.

Establishing Clear Goals and Roles

Once you have assembled the team, establish clear goals and roles. Each team member should understand their responsibilities and how their role contributes to the larger objectives of the team and the organization. This clarity prevents overlap and confusion, allowing team members to focus on their strengths and contributions.

Fostering Open Communication

Open and honest communication is the essence of a cohesive team. Encourage a culture where team members feel comfortable sharing their thoughts, ideas, and concerns (Antrobus & Antrobus, 2023). Regular team meetings, open-door policies, and team-building activities can help foster this environment. Remember, effective communication involves not only speaking but also listening – be an active listener and encourage others to do the same.

Building Trust and Respect

Trust and respect are vital ingredients of team cohesion. These are built over time through consistent, fair, and respectful interactions. Lead by example – show respect in your interactions, keep your commitments, and be transparent in your decision-making. Devising opportunities for team members to collaborate on tasks and projects can also strengthen trust and interdependence.

Encouraging Collaboration and Teamwork

Finally, encourage collaboration and teamwork. Promote a team mentality where success is celebrated collectively rather than individually. Recognize and reward teamwork and collaborative achievements. Team-building exercises and collaborative projects can also solidify the sense of teamwork.

Think of your team as an ensemble, each member with unique skills and perspectives. The key to creating a cohesive team is understanding and harmonizing these individual differences towards a common goal. Start by selecting team members based on skills and their fit into the team's culture and dynamics. Encourage a sense of belonging where each member feels valued and understood. Set clear goals and roles, ensuring everyone knows what is expected of them and how they contribute to the team's success. Remember, a cohesive team is one where diversity is celebrated and unity is cultivated through mutual respect and shared objectives.

Fostering Team Collaboration and Morale: The Leader's Symphony

A key leadership responsibility is fostering an environment where collaboration thrives and morale remains high. This environment not only enhances productivity but also makes the workplace a more enjoyable and fulfilling place. Here are some techniques to encourage teamwork and maintain high morale in your team.

Promote a Collaborative Environment

Create a work culture that values and rewards collaboration. Motivate the team to share ideas, work on projects, and support each other's efforts. Consider setting up collaborative workspaces, using team-based project management tools, or encouraging open discussions where everyone's input is valued. Recognize and celebrate collaborative efforts to reinforce their importance.

Encourage Positive Relationships

Positive interpersonal relationships are the bedrock of team collaboration and high morale. Foster an environment where team members get to know and understand each other beyond professional roles. Manage this through team-building activities, social events, or informal gatherings. When team members connect personally, they are more likely to communicate effectively, trust, and work well together.

Provide Opportunities for Growth and Development

People are more engaged and motivated when they feel they are growing and developing in their roles. Provide your team members opportunities to acquire new skills, take on new challenges, or advance in their careers. Include training sessions and mentorship programs or assign them to new projects that stretch their abilities.

Maintain Open and Transparent Communication

Keep the lines of communication open and transparent. Regularly update your team on company news, project progress, and any changes that may affect them. Encourage feedback and be open to suggestions from team members. When people feel informed and heard, they are more engaged and have higher morale.

Recognize and Appreciate Efforts

Recognition and appreciation can significantly boost morale. Acknowledge your team's hard work and achievements individually and in groups. Remember, it does not always have to be through formal rewards; often, a simple thank you or public acknowledgment can be very effective.

Manage Workload Effectively

Overwork and stress can quickly erode teamwork and morale. Monitor your team's workload to ensure it is manageable. Provide support where needed and be flexible, understanding that sometimes personal circumstances can affect work performance.

The morale of your team is the melody of your leadership symphony. Foster an environment where collaboration is the norm and morale is high. Here, you will create opportunities for team members to collaborate, share ideas, and learn from each other. Encourage open communication, recognize achievements, and celebrate milestones. Address conflicts promptly and fairly, ensuring they do not fester and affect team morale. Remember, high morale is not just about happiness; Create an atmosphere where team members are motivated, engaged, and committed to the team's objectives.

Delegating Effectively: The Leader's Trust

Effective delegation for a leader is a crucial skill. It is not just about offloading tasks to free up your time; it is about empowering your team, building trust, and focusing on strategic leadership responsibilities.

Understanding when and how to delegate is vital to being an effective leader.

Identifying Tasks to Delegate

Start by identifying tasks that you can delegate. These are typically tasks that do not require your specific expertise or decision-making authority. Look for ones that can provide developmental opportunities for your team members. Delegating these not only helps you focus on higher-level responsibilities but also aids in the growth and development of your team.

Choosing the Right Person

Once you have identified tasks to delegate, choose the right person for the job next. Consider the skills, interests, and developmental needs of your team members. Match the task to the individual who has the appropriate skills or who would benefit most from the learning opportunity. This thoughtful approach ensures that delegation is effective and beneficial for both the team and the individual.

Providing Clear Instructions and Expectations

When delegating, be clear about what you expect. Provide detailed instructions, the desired outcome, and the deadline. Ensure the team member understands the task and has the necessary resources and authority to complete it. Clarity at the outset prevents confusion and ensures the task is completed as expected.

Empowering and Trusting Your Team

Delegation is an act of trust. Empower your team members by giving them the autonomy to complete the task in their own way. Avoid micromanaging, which can undermine trust and stifle innovation. Trust that your team members will come to you if they need support or guidance.

Providing Support and Feedback

While giving your team autonomy is essential, it is also crucial to be available to provide support and answer questions. Encourage an open line of communication and be approachable. After the task is completed, provide constructive feedback. Take this opportunity for you and the team member to learn and grow.

Review and Adjust

Finally, regularly review the effectiveness of your delegation. Are tasks being completed satisfactorily? Are team members growing and developing their skills? Be prepared to adjust your approach based on what is or is not working.

Delegation is not just a task management tool but an act of trust and empowerment. It is recognizing the strengths of your team members and giving them the autonomy to use those strengths. Effective delegation involves clearly defining tasks, providing the necessary resources, and setting expectations for outcomes. It also means being available for guidance and support without micromanaging. Trust your team; they will deliver and rise to the occasion. Effective delegation frees up your time for strategic leadership tasks while fostering growth and development within your team.

As we wrap up this chapter, reflect on the power of a well-built and well-led team. This cornerstone of effective leadership is a testament to your ability to unite, inspire, and guide.

The next chapter, "Navigating Challenges and Conflict," will take you through the strategies to handle challenges and conflicts that arise in any team setting, equipping you with the tools to maintain harmony and forward momentum.

5

Navigating Challenges and Conflict

L eadership is about steering the ship in calm waters and navigating through storms. This chapter delves into recognizing and addressing the challenges and conflicts that are part and parcel of team dynamics and leading effectively through change and uncertainty.

Identifying and Addressing Team Challenges: The Leader's Diagnostic

In any team environment, challenges and issues are inevitable. As a leader, your ability to identify and address these challenges effectively is crucial for maintaining a productive and harmonious team. This section focuses on strategies for recognizing typical team issues and implementing solutions.

Recognizing the Signs of Team Challenges

The first step in addressing team challenges is to recognize them. Common signs include missed deadlines, declining quality of work, frequent misunderstandings or communication breakdowns, low morale, and lack of engagement. Stay attuned to changes in team dynamics and individual behaviors, as these can be early indicators of underlying issues.

Creating an Open Feedback Culture

Foster an environment where team members feel comfortable sharing their concerns and feedback. Regular check-ins and open discussions encourage team members to voice issues before they escalate. This open dialogue can provide valuable insights into the root causes of team challenges.

Analyzing the Underlying Causes

Once a challenge is identified, analyze its underlying causes. Is it due to a lack of clear communication, conflicting personalities, insufficient resources, or unaligned goals? Understanding the root cause is necessary for developing an effective solution.

Implementing Targeted Solutions

Based on your analysis, implement solutions that address the specific challenges your team is facing. For instance, if miscommunication is an issue, improve your communication channels or provide training on effective communication. Consider team-building activities or conflict resolution training if conflicts arise from personality clashes.

Involving the Team in Problem-Solving

Involve your team in the problem-solving process. This empowers the team and provides diverse perspectives for a more comprehensive solution. Collaborative problem-solving can also enhance team cohesion and buy-in for the implemented solutions.

Monitoring Progress and Adjusting as Needed

After implementing solutions, monitor the team's progress. Check if the measures effectively resolve the issues or if additional adjustments are needed. Be flexible and ready to make changes as necessary.

Providing Support and Resources

Ensure your team has the support and resources they need to overcome challenges. Consider providing additional training, adjusting workloads, or bringing in other resources.

Every team faces its set of challenges, from miscommunication to mismatched goals. As a leader, developing a keen eye for these challenges is crucial. Begin by fostering an environment where team members feel comfortable voicing concerns. Regular check-ins and open communication channels can help you spot issues before they escalate. Once identified, address these challenges head-on. Tailor your approach to each situation, whether it requires a team meeting, a one-on-one conversation, or a shift in team dynamics. Remember, the key is not just to solve the problem but to learn from it and strengthen the team.

Conflict Resolution: The Leader's Peacekeeping Mission

Conflict resolution is vital for any leader, as conflicts, if not managed constructively, can disrupt team harmony and productivity. Effective conflict resolution involves addressing disagreements quickly and fairly, ensuring they are resolved in a way that strengthens the team. Here are vital techniques to manage and resolve conflicts constructively.

Encourage Open Dialogue

When a conflict arises, encourage open dialogue. Create a safe environment where everyone involved can express views without fear of judgment or reprisal. This open communication is the first step towards understanding the different perspectives involved in the conflict.

Active Listening

Practice active listening. Entirely concentrating on what is being said rather than just passively hearing the speaker's message. Active listening involves acknowledging, summarizing, and reflecting on what is said. This approach helps clarify misunderstandings and shows respect for the opinions of others.

Identify the Root Cause

Get to the heart of the conflict by identifying its root cause. Conflicts often stem from underlying issues such as unmet needs, differing values, or miscommunication. Understanding the true source of the conflict is essential for finding a lasting resolution.

Focus on Interests, Not Positions

Encourage those involved to focus on interests, not positions. Instead of clinging to their stance, they should express the underlying reasons for their views. This approach opens up the possibility of finding a mutually acceptable solution.

Find Common Ground

Look for areas of agreement or common ground. Starting from the point of agreement can set a positive tone for the discussion and make it easier to address areas of disagreement.

Develop Win-Win Solutions

Aim for a win-win solution where both parties feel their concerns have been addressed. Brainstorm possible solutions and evaluate these options until a mutually beneficial resolution is found.

Agree on a Way Forward

Once a solution is agreed upon, outline each party's steps to implement the resolution. Clear action steps and deadlines help resolve the conflict and prevent similar issues.

Follow Up

After the conflict is resolved, follow up with those involved. This follow-up can help ensure that the agreed-upon actions are being taken and that no new issues have emerged.

Conflict within a team is inevitable, but how it is managed can make all the difference. For conflict resolution, focus on a mindset of finding a win-win solution that respects and values each party's perspective. Encourage open and respectful dialogue, and be an active listener. Your role is to mediate and guide the discussion towards a constructive resolution, not to dictate it. Sometimes, turning a conflict into a collaborative problem-solving session takes a new perspective. Successfully resolved conflicts can lead to deeper understanding and more robust team bonds.

Adapting to Change and Uncertainty: The Leader's Compass in the Storm

Leading effectively through times of change and uncertainty is vital. In today's fast-paced world, adaptability and resilience are crucial to navigating the inevitable shifts and surprises that come your way. Here is how you can guide your team through these periods with confidence and clarity.

Embrace Change as an Opportunity

Begin by reframing how you view change. Instead of seeing it as an obstacle, view it as an opportunity for growth and innovation. This mindset can help you approach change with a positive attitude, which can inspire and motivate your team.

Communicate Openly and Frequently

During times of change, effective communication becomes even more crucial. Keep your team informed about what changes are happening, why they are occurring, and how they will impact the team. Be transparent about what you know and what you do not know. Regular updates can help reduce uncertainty and speculation, which can be unsettling for team members.

Encourage Flexibility and Agility

The team should be flexible and agile, with the leader's encouragement. Consider adjusting to new processes, adopting new technologies, or shifting team roles. Help your team understand that adaptability is valuable and that being open to change is crucial for personal and professional development.

Provide Support and Resources

Changes can be challenging, and providing your team with the support and resources they need to adjust is important. Consider additional training, frequent check-ins, or listening to their concerns and suggestions.

Lead by Example

Demonstrate your adaptability and resilience. Your team will look to you for cues on how to react to changes. You can set the tone for your team's response by staying calm, focused, and positive.

Foster a Culture of Continuous Learning

Encourage a culture where continuous learning and development are valued. Help your team remain equipped and confident to handle changes. Promote the idea that skill development and adaptability are ongoing processes.

Involve the Team in Decision-Making

Whenever possible, involve your team in decision-making processes during times of change. Help them feel more in control and invested in the outcome. It also allows for a diversity of ideas and solutions to be considered.

Celebrate Adaptability and Resilience

Finally, recognize and celebrate instances where your team adapts well to change. Acknowledging their flexibility and resilience can reinforce these behaviors and encourage a positive attitude toward future changes.

Change is the only constant, and uncertainty can often be unsettling. Leading a team through these times requires a blend of steadfastness and flexibility. Communicate changes transparently, focusing on the 'why' behind them. Be open to feedback and concerns, and be prepared to adapt your strategies as needed. Your confidence and calm demeanor can provide stability for the team. Encourage adaptability and resilience, reinforcing the notion that change, while challenging, can also bring opportunities for growth and innovation.

As this chapter concludes, remember that the challenges and conflicts you face as a leader are not roadblocks but opportunities to strengthen and refine your leadership skills and your team.

In the next chapter, "Growth and Continuous Improvement," we will explore how to foster an environment of ongoing development for yourself and your team, ensuring that your leadership journey is one of constant evolution and betterment.

6

Growth and Continuous Improvement

I n the realm of leadership, the pursuit of growth and improvement is never-ending. This chapter is dedicated to self-enhancement and preparation for future leadership roles, focusing on self-reflection, feedback, mentorship, and professional development.

Self-Reflection and Feedback: The Leader's Mirror

Self-reflection and feedback are crucial to personal growth, especially in leadership. Utilizing these tools effectively can significantly enhance your self-awareness, decision-making, and leadership abilities. Here is how to incorporate self-reflection and feedback into your leadership growth.

Regular Self-Reflection

Regularly plan time for self-reflection. Find the time at the end of each day, week, or after a major project or event. During this time, assess your actions, decisions, and interactions. Ask yourself questions like: What did I handle well? What could I have done differently? What did I learn? This process helps you to understand your strengths and areas for improvement.

Maintain a Reflection Journal

Consider keeping a reflection journal. Writing down your thoughts, feelings, and observations about your leadership experiences can provide insights into your personal growth. It also helps in processing complex situations and can be a valuable resource to look back on.

Seeking and Welcoming Feedback

Actively seek feedback from your team, peers, and superiors (Weber, 2023). Create an environment where feedback is valued as a tool for improvement, not criticism. When receiving feedback, listen attentively, ask clarifying questions, and resist the urge to defend your actions. Remember, the goal is to understand and improve, not to justify.

Analyzing Feedback

Take time to analyze the feedback you receive. Look for common themes or areas that multiple people have pointed out. This provides valuable insights into how others perceive your leadership and areas where you can improve.

Setting Personal Development Goals

Use the insights gained from self-reflection and feedback to set personal development goals. Identify areas you want to improve and plan how to achieve these improvements. Including reading books, attending workshops, or seeking mentorship in particular areas of leadership.

Acting on Feedback

Finally, act on the feedback you receive. Make conscious efforts to incorporate the insights into your leadership practice. Look at changing certain behaviors, improving communication skills, or being more open to new ideas.

Regularly Reviewing Your Growth

Periodically review your progress against your personal development goals. Reflect on how your changes impact your leadership and adjust your goals and strategies as necessary.

The journey to becoming an effective and influential leader starts with looking inward. Self-reflection is your mirror, offering insights into your strengths, weaknesses, and areas for growth. Make it a regular practice to assess your leadership style and decisions. What worked? What did not? Why? Complement this introspection with feedback from peers, superiors, and team members. Embrace feedback, even when challenging, as a tool for learning and improvement. This dual approach of self-reflection and openness to feedback creates a powerful engine for personal growth and leadership development.

Mentorship and Professional Development: The Leader's Pathway

Pursuing mentorship and continuous professional development is essential for any leader aiming to grow and excel in their role. These elements enhance your skills and knowledge and provide new perspectives and insights crucial for effective leadership.

Seeking Mentorship

Actively seek out mentorship opportunities. A mentor, especially one with experience in leadership, can provide guidance, advice, and support. They can help you navigate the complexities of your role, offer perspectives based on their experiences, and encourage you when facing challenges. Look for mentors both within your organization and in the broader professional community. Mentor relationships can be formal or informal and should be based on mutual respect and a genuine desire for growth.

Being Open to Different Perspectives

A key benefit of mentorship is gaining insights from someone with a different perspective. Be open to your mentor's advice and feedback, even if it challenges your existing beliefs or approaches. This openness can lead to significant personal and professional growth.

Ongoing Learning and Development

In addition to mentorship, commit to ongoing learning and development. The leadership landscape constantly evolves, and staying informed about new theories, practices, and skills is crucial. Consider participating in workshops, attending conferences, enrolling in courses, or even pursuing further academic qualifications related to leadership.

Leveraging Online Resources

Take advantage of online resources and platforms for learning. Numerous webinars, online courses, podcasts, and articles on leadership and management are available. Integrate these resources into your daily routine and provide flexibility in your learning.

Networking and Professional Groups

Engage with professional groups and networks related to leadership. These groups can be valuable resources for learning from peers, sharing experiences, and staying updated on industry trends. Networking will open doors to new opportunities and collaborations.

Applying Learning to Practice

As you learn, look for ways to apply new knowledge and skills to your leadership practice. Experiment with new leadership styles, implement new strategies within your team or even initiate new projects.

Encouraging Team Learning

Lastly, encourage a culture of learning within your team. Share what you know and encourage your team members to pursue their own professional development. Enhancing the overall capability of your team and fostering an environment of continuous improvement.

No leader grows in isolation. The guidance of a mentor can be invaluable in navigating the complexities of leadership. Seek out mentors who embody the qualities you aspire to and can provide wisdom gleaned from their experiences. Alongside mentorship, invest in your professional development. Attend workshops, enroll in courses, or stay aware of the latest trends and best practices in leadership. Continuous learning is about accumulating knowledge and staying adaptable, relevant, and prepared for challenges.

Preparing for Future Leadership Roles: The Leader's Vision

As you grow in your current leadership position, it is essential to also prepare for future, more advanced leadership opportunities. This preparation is about enhancing your existing skills and expanding your vision and understanding of what it takes to lead at higher levels.

Develop a Long-Term Career Vision

Start by developing a long-term vision for your career. Where do you see yourself in five, ten, or fifteen years? What kind of leadership roles do you aspire to hold? Having a clear vision of your future helps guide your decisions and actions in the present. It keeps you focused on the end goal and motivates you to push your boundaries continuously.

Expand Your Leadership Skills

While you may have mastered specific skills in your current role, higher leadership positions require a broader skill set. Work on developing skills critical for advanced leadership roles, such as strategic thinking, change management, and high-level decision-making. Include taking on projects outside your comfort zone, seeking additional responsibilities, or engaging in cross-functional collaboration.

Build a Diverse Network

Cultivate a diverse professional network. Connect with individuals both within and outside your industry. Networking with various professionals can provide insights into different leadership styles and strategies and inform you about potential leadership opportunities.

Seek Feedback and Mentorship

Continue to seek feedback on your leadership style and decisions. Regular feedback helps you understand how others perceive your leadership and highlights areas for improvement. Additionally, seek mentorship from leaders in positions where you aspire to be. Their guidance can be invaluable in helping you navigate your path to advanced leadership roles.

Stay Informed and Adaptable

Stay informed about trends, industry changes, and the broader business environment. Understanding these dynamics can help you adapt your leadership approach to meet future challenges and remain relevant in an ever-changing world.

Invest in Continued Education

Consider furthering your education through formal degrees, leadership courses, or specialized training programs. Continued education can deepen your knowledge, sharpen your skills, and demonstrate your commitment to your professional development.

Embrace Leadership Opportunities

Whenever possible, embrace opportunities to demonstrate your leadership abilities, especially in high-visibility or high-stakes situations. These opportunities can be platforms to showcase your capability to handle advanced leadership roles.

Reflect and Adjust Your Plan

Regularly reflect on your progress toward your future leadership goals. Be open to adjusting your plan as necessary – new experiences, challenges, and opportunities can shape your path in unexpected yet beneficial ways.

Preparing for future leadership opportunities is essential as you grow in your current role. While Excelling in your present responsibilities, you must develop skills and knowledge for higher levels of leadership. Think about the broader impact you want to have and the kind of leader you aspire to become. Set goals for your leadership journey and create a roadmap for achieving them. Take on challenging projects, expand your network, or build expertise in areas beyond your current role. Remember, preparing for future leadership roles is about laying the groundwork today for the impact you want to have tomorrow.

As we conclude this chapter, reflect on your journey of growth and continuous improvement. Leadership is constantly learning, adapting, and evolving (Admin, 2023). Embrace this journey with an open heart and mind, and let your leadership growth be a testament to your commitment to excellence and impact.

In the next and final chapter, "Conclusion," we will summarize the key takeaways from this book and leave you with final thoughts to inspire your continued journey in leadership.

7

Conclusion: The Leader's Path Forward

As we draw the curtains on this journey through "Essential Leadership Skills: The Path to Effectiveness, Influence, and Growth," let us pause to reflect on your path. From understanding the nuanced difference between a manager and a leader to mastering critical skills like communication, decision-making, and time management, this guide has been a compass in navigating the complex waters of leadership.

The book explored the art of building and nurturing teams, embracing the challenges and conflicts that come with team dynamics, and the continuous pursuit of growth and improvement. Each chapter was a step towards being a leader, not only in title but also in action and impact. Effective, influential leadership is a journey, not a destination. It is about constant learning, adapting, and growing.

As you step forward from here, carry the lessons learned and the insights gained. Let them guide you to face new challenges, make tough decisions, and inspire those you lead. Embrace the responsibility of leadership with courage and empathy, knowing that the path you are on is one of profound impact and fulfillment.

I encourage you to continue your development, to seek new knowledge, and to approach every challenge as an opportunity to grow. As you move forward, I invite you to share your experience. If this book has guided you, enlightened you, or inspired you in your leadership journey, please take a moment to leave a review on Amazon. Your feedback not only supports my work but also helps other aspiring leaders find their path to effective leadership.

The journey of leadership is ongoing, and the world needs skilled, compassionate, visionary, and resilient leaders. Be that leader. Your team, your organization, and the world await your impact.

8

Resources

- Admin. (2023, August 23). *The art of Effective leadership: Inspiring your small business team*. Ascend Business Mastermind. https://goas cend.biz/the-art-of-effective-leadership-inspiring-your-small-b usiness-team/.
- Antrobus, D., & Antrobus, D. (2023, July 24). Empowering teams for success | Dave Antrobus. *Dave Antrobus - Co-founder and Group CTO of Inc & Co*. https://daveantrobus.com/the-human-element-in-tur narounds-empowering- teams-for-success/
- Beez, D., & Beez, D. (2023, May 3). Developing leadership skills: inspiring and motivating others. *TS PUBLISHING*. https://tspublishi ng.us/growth/developing-leadership-skills-inspiring-and-motiva ting-others/
- *How can I improve my assertiveness and communication skills in a leadership position?* (n.d.). List of What. https://listofwhat.com/ questions-answers/how-can-i-improve-my-assertiveness-and-c ommunication-skills-in-a-leadership-position.
- OpenAI. (2024). *ChatGPT (4) [Large language model]*. https://chat.op enai.com.

- *Strategies for Effective Decision-Making in Leadership Roles.* (n.d.). Priority Management. https://www.prioritymanagement.com/ll-ne wsletter/strategies-for-effective-decision-making-in-leadership-roles
- Team, M. (2023, September 6). 7 Essential qualities of a great leader and how to develop them. *missconsult.* https://www.missconsult.co m/post/7-essential-qualities-of-a-great-leader-and-how-to-dev elop-them.
- Unitive. (2023, July 19). *Unmasking Self-Deception: Overcoming the Hidden Barrier to Effective Leadership - Unitive.* https://unitive.org/bl og/unmasking-self-deception-overcoming-the-hidden-barrier-t o-effective-leadership/
- *Unlocking success: Building strong project governance and Decision-Making structures for effective execution – SOJECT.* (n.d.). https://sojec t.com/unlocking-success-building-strong-project-governance-a nd-decision-making-structures-for effective-execution/
- Weber. (2023, November 10). *Unleashing the Power of Communication: A 10-point Guide for High-Performance Leaders.* Communication Coach | Executive Coach. https://drwebercoaching.com/unleash ing-the-power-of-communication-a-10-point-guide-for-high-p erformance-leaders/